AF488207

Some of us are Ghosts

Written and Illustrated by
Sandra Russell

Monday Creek Publishing
Ohio USA

To Chloe

Some of us are ghosts;
walking in night roads

The mist of our dreams,
our only bodies

The waltzing of trees
is our crowd

Some of us are Ghosts

We sway like metronomes counting

We sigh that the clocks
have stopped adding

The wind is a carpet we•re riding

There•s nobody ringing the bells

Some of us are ghosts

The meadow•s returning the echo

The ending is where we begin

A feather•s a flight,
for the birds of the night

Till the dawn and the dew draws us in

Some of us are ghosts

We murmur the songs of the living

Our hearts carry secrets to tell

Like pearls in a wave no net catching

On a road paved with tumbling shells

Some of us are ghosts

About the Author

Sandra Russell was born about 100 feet from the spot in the road that would become this poem's inspiration. Sandra was recognized as an "artist" by family members before school age, and employed by teachers in elementary school to draw ponies for the other kids to color, eventually earning degrees in the fine arts in sculpture and art history. Sandra enjoys cooking, musical theater, and doing puzzles.